Rookie Read-About™ Science

So That's How the Moon Changes Shape!

By Allan Fowler

Consultants:
Robert L. Hillerich, Ph.D., Bowling Green
State University, Bowling Green, Ohio

Mary Nalbandian, Director of Science,
Chicago Public Schools, Chicago, Illinois

Fay Robinson, Child Development Specialist

CHILDRENS PRESS®
CHICAGO

Series cover and interior design by Sara Shelton

Library of Congress Cataloging-in-Publication Data

Fowler, Allan.
    So that's how the moon changes shape / by Allan Fowler.
        p. cm. — (Rookie read-about science)
    Summary: A simple explanation of the moon and why it changes shape
throughout the month.
        ISBN 0-516-04917-8
        1. Moon—Phases—Juvenile literature. [1.   Moon] I. Title.
    II. Series: Fowler, Allan. Rookie read-about science.
QB588.F68   1991
523.3—dc20   91-3142
                                                                          CIP
                                                                          AC

10 11 12 13 14 15 16 17 18 R 02 01 00

Do you ever look up at the moon and wonder, "Why can't the moon make up its mind what shape to be in?"

4

Sometimes the moon is a bright circle, and we call it a full moon.

But some nights the moon looks more like this...

or like this half moon...

or like this crescent.

And some nights...
you can't see it at all!

How does the moon
change its shape?

It doesn't!

It's always a big ball...

14

a ball of rock with neither
air nor water—so people
and animals and plants
can't live there.

But you see only the part of the moon that's lit. The rest is too dark to see. Yet it's there!

17

Why doesn't the whole
moon shine every night?

19

Because the moon doesn't really shine at all!

It's the sun that shines on the moon and lights it up. We say that the moon reflects the sunlight.

Even though the sun is on the other side of the Earth at night, where you can't see it, the sun's rays may still reach the moon and make it glow.

23

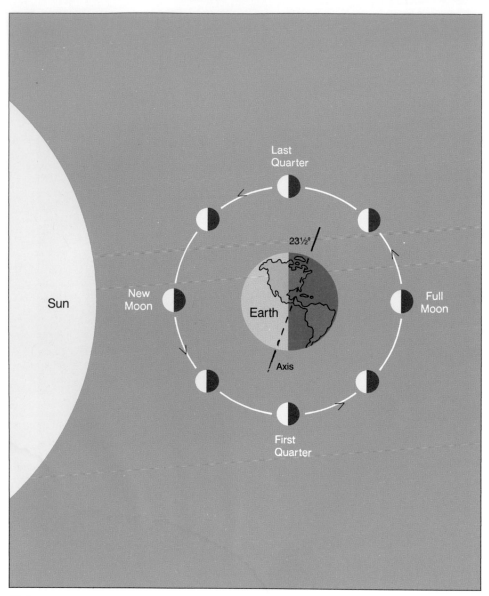

Sun

Last
Quarter

23½°

New
Moon

Earth

Full
Moon

Axis

First
Quarter

24

The moon is always traveling in a big circle around the Earth.

Depending on where
the sun and moon are
in the sky, we may see
some of the moon,
all of the moon,
or none of the moon
lit up by the sun.

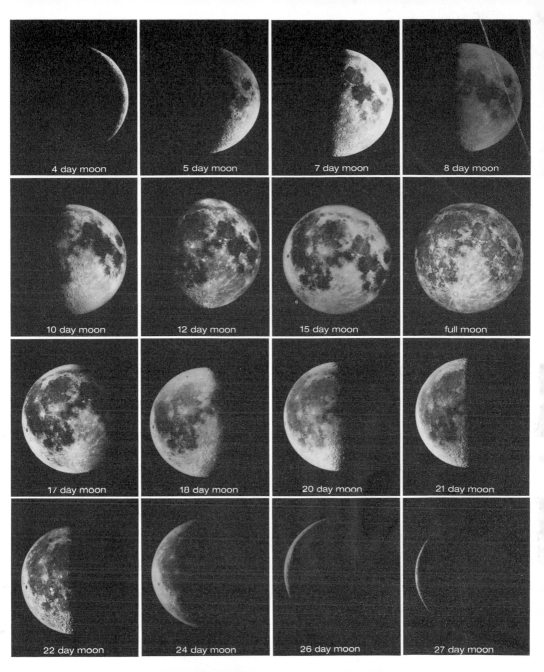

So that's how the moon seems to change its shape!

Next time you think you see the moon shining, remember you're really looking at sunshine!

Words You Know

moon

full moon

half moon

crescent moon

30

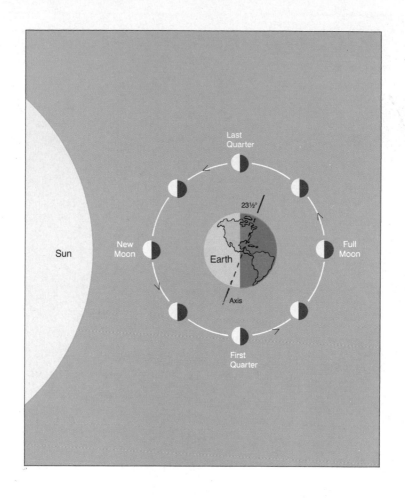

So that's how the
moon changes shape!

Index

About the Author

Allan Fowler is a free-lance writer with a background in advertising. Born in New York, he lives in Chicago now and enjoys traveling.

Photo Credits

NASA—14, 15, 20, 23

PhotoEdit—© Debby Davis, 3

Valan—© J. R. Page, 4, 30 (top left); © J. Eastcott/Y. Momatiuk, 7; © Kennon Cooke, 8; © Gilles DeLisle, 10; © John Fowler, 13; © S. J. Krasemann, 17, 19; © Dr. A. Farquhar, 28; © Francis Lépine, 30 (top right); © Val Wilkinson, 30 (bottom right)

Yerkes Observatory Photograph—Cover (4 photos), 27 (16 photos)

Art by Chuck Hills—24, 31

COVER: 4 day moon, 7 day moon, 14 day moon, 24 day moon